Two by Two

Barbara Reid

Scholastic Inc.

New York

For my family
and the H. M.

*The illustrations for this book were made with Plasticine that is shaped
and pressed onto illustration board. Acrylic glaze or paint is used
for shiny or metallic effects.*

Photography by Ian Crysler

Originally published in Canada in 1992 by Scholastic Canada Ltd.

Library of Congress Cataloging-in-Publication Data

Reid, Barbara.
    Two by two / by Barbara Reid.
        p.   cm.
    Summary: A retelling in verse of the Old Testament story about
the survival of Noah, his family, and animals during forty days
and nights of rain.
    ISBN 0-590-45869-8
    1. Noah's ark—Juvenile literature. 2. Deluge—Juvenile
literature. [1. Noah's ark. 2. Bible stories—O.T.] I. Title.
BS658.R44   1993
222'.1109505—dc20   92-9013
                                                          CIP
                                                           AC

12 11 10 9 8 7 6 5 4 3 2 1   3 4 5 6 7 8/9

Printed in Hong Kong

First Scholastic printing, April 1993

Way back in the olden days
People turned to evil ways.
They spoiled the world with greedy plots,
Dirty deeds and nasty thoughts.

 God was mad, and with a frown,
Said, "Wash it clean! Let them drown!"

There were some things God thought to save,
He'd need the help of someone brave.

"*Noah!* You're both good and kind,
I'll tell you what I have in mind . . . "

So Noah came to build an ark
With pine tar, string and hickory bark.

He made it long and tall and wide
With room for two of each inside.

Mrs. Noah gathered seed
From every flower, tree and weed.

6

Three sons brought food for one and all,
Their wives packed more and piled it tall.

Just in time
the job was done;
The family boarded one by one.

7

Then in came the animals two by two,
The frogs leaped over a kangaroo.

And in came the animals three by three,
The fleas rode in on a chimpanzee.

9

Now in came the animals four by four,
Pushing and squeezing to get in the door.

Then in came the animals
five by five,
The ark was as busy
as a big beehive.

And in came the animals six by six,
Pandas and penguins, all in a mix.

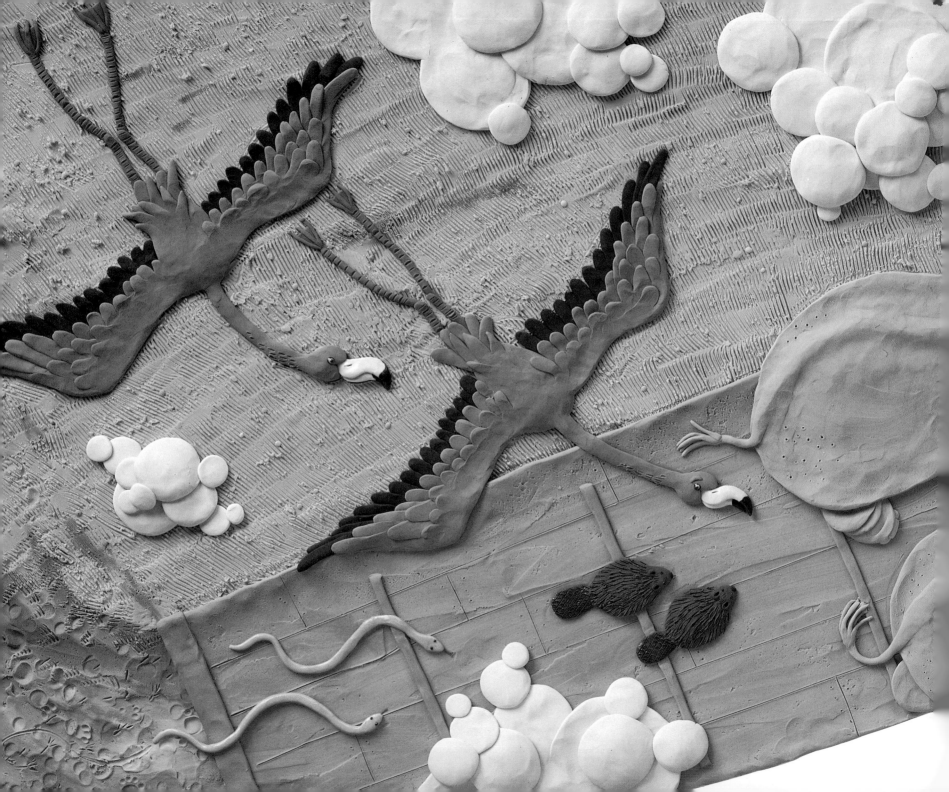

Now in came the animals seven by seven,
A drop of rain fell out of heaven.

15

Then in came the animals
eight by eight,
Each cat paced
beside its mate.

And in came the animals
nine by nine,
Watch out for
that porcupine!

17

18   Now in came the animals ten by ten,

The sloths slunk slowly on, and then . . .

"*All aboard!*" cried Noah,
"*Shut the door!*"
And down came the rain
as never before.
The sky had sprung
so many leaks
That whales swam over
mountain peaks.

For forty days and nights it poured,
Inside the ark the possums snored.

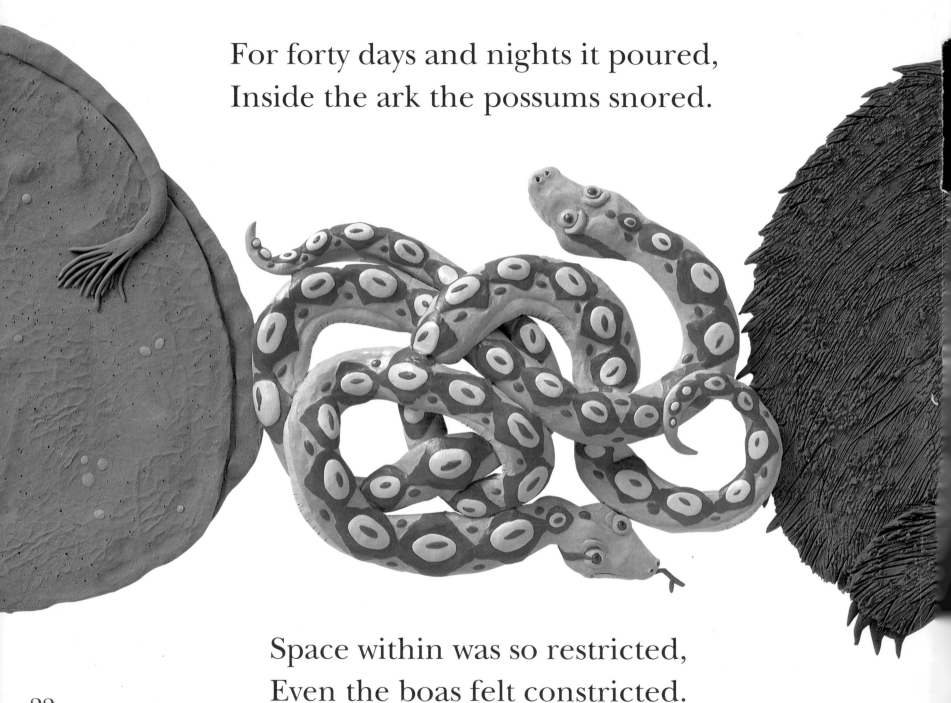

Space within was so restricted,
Even the boas felt constricted.

22

One happy day the rain was done;
The bats hung blinking in the sun.

Noah said to Raven: "Fly!
Try to find a spot that's dry!"

A week went by without a word,
So Noah sent another bird.

The dove returned, to great relief:
"Look here, I've brought an olive leaf!
And since the ark has come to rest,
I think I'll go and build a nest."

Noah offered up his thanks,
Opened the door and lowered the planks.

With hoot and squawk and squeak and bark,
The animals tumbled off the ark.

God gave the rainbow as a sign
That after rain the sun will shine.

28

Seasons and days shall never cease,
And then God told them, "Grow in peace."

Tune and chorus: traditional
Verses by Barbara Reid

CHORUS

Medium fast

Well, who built the ark? No - ah, No - ah.

Who built the ark? Broth - er No - ah built the ark.
(to verses)

VERSES

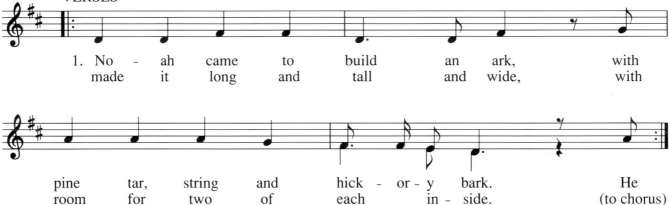

1. No - ah came to build an ark, with
made it long and tall and wide, with

pine tar, string and hick - or - y bark. He
room for two of each in - side. (to chorus)

1. Noah came to build an ark
   With pine tar, string and hickory bark.
   He made it long and tall and wide
   With room for two of each inside.

2. Then in came the animals two by two,
   The frogs leaped over a kangaroo.
   And in came the animals three by three,
   The fleas rode in on a chimpanzee.

3. Now in came the animals four by four,
   Pushing and squeezing to get in the door.
   Then in came the animals five by five,
   The ark was as busy as a big beehive.

4. In came the animals six by six,
   Pandas and penguins, all in a mix.
   And in came the animals seven by seven,
   A drop of rain fell out of heaven.

5. Then in came the animals eight by eight,
   Each cat paced beside its mate.
   And in came the animals nine by nine,
   Watch out for that porcupine!

6. Now in came the animals ten by ten,
   The sloths slunk slowly on, and then . . .
   "All aboard!" cried Noah, "Shut the door!"
   And down came the rain as never before.